SEX AND RELATIONSHIPS

SIX YOUTH GROUP SESSIONS FROM GENESIS, ROMANS, 1 CORINTHIANS & EPHESIANS

ROGER FAWCETT

CF4•K

10 9 8 7 6 5 4 3 2 1

ISBN: 978-1-84550-549-3

Edited by David Jackman and Thalia Blundell

Published in 2010 by

Christian Focus Publications, Geanies House, Fearn,

Tain, Ross-shire, IV20 1TW, Great Britain.

www.christianfocus.com

Cover design by Daniel van Straaten

Printed by Bell and Bain, Glasgow

*Worksheets are reproducible.
Each youth leader should have their own copy of this book.

CONTENTS

INTRODUCTION

BY NICK MARGESSON

As a youth leader you have the great privilege of introducing young people to the Lord Jesus Christ and helping them to grow in the Christian faith. The 14-18s age group are at the junction between the younger teens and the adult church and this is often where we lose them. *The Junction* is a series of books designed to help you teach older teens to study the Bible in a way which is challenging and intellectually stretching. Because they are often unprepared to take things at face value and are encouraged to question everything, it is important to satisfy the mind while touching the heart. The ready-to-use sessions contained in the books are for youth groups of varying sizes, with normal leaders and normal teenagers who want to serve an awesome God.

Each book in the series contains one teaching module, which will normally last from 4-7 weeks. At the front of the book is an overview of the Bible teaching, which can be photocopied for your church leader so that he/she is aware of what is being taught. Each lesson plan, in addition to a lesson aim, contains study notes to enable the leader to understand the Bible passage, a slot to encourage the young people to share experiences and learn from each other, a suggestion to focus attention on the study to follow, suggestions for a prayer and praise time and an optional worksheet to help the young people engage with the passage. Recognising that youth groups vary in size and available space every effort has been made to include activities that are easily adaptable.

Putting Together a Youth Group Session

What should we include in our youth group sessions?

If you wander into any Christian bookshop and ask the question, "What should we include in our youth group sessions?" you had better be prepared for a very long stay in the bookshop! Just about every book on youth ministry that you pick up off the shelf will give you a different answer to that question – generally based on the author's preference, upbringing, experiences, etc. Interestingly, if you pick up your Bible and ask the same question you will also be in for a long wait, because, as far as I can see, the Bible never mentions youth groups, let alone what might be involved in a youth group session. In fact, the Bible very rarely makes any distinction between particular groupings of Christians – it talks about all Christians and makes no particular distinction about age or nationality or background, etc.

So, if our youth group is a Christian youth group, then the question we really need to ask is, "What does it look like when Christians (of any age) get together?" And, on this subject, the Bible has plenty to say! One of the most complete descriptions of what this looks like in practice comes in Acts 2:42-47, where we are given a fairly detailed description of what the earliest group of believers was like. Whenever God's people got together, they engaged in a whole variety of activities – they prayed together, they praised God together, they learned from God's word together, they reminded each other of what God had done for them, they cared practically for each other, they spent plenty of time together, they cared for the world around them, they proclaimed the good news of Jesus, and so on. You could sum it up by saying that they were devoted to God and devoted to each other. And, interestingly, this type of devotion was clearly very attractive to the world around them – 'the Lord added to their number daily those who were being saved' (Acts 2:47).

If our youth group is a Christian youth group then, in a youth appropriate way, we need to be displaying that same devotion to God and to each other whenever we meet together. What elements in our youth group sessions will help our groups to do this?

- **Time** – it is noticeable in Acts 2 how much time the early believers spent together. They met together daily in the temple courts, they ate together, they hung out at each others' homes.

  With busy teenagers and busy leaders, spending this much time together would be impossible for just about every youth group, but relationships are a key element of being devoted to one another, and relationships need time and space to develop. In our programming we need to allow time and space for young people and leaders to hang out together.

  Food is a great way to get people to spend time together and, again, it does not have to be complicated or fancy – a bag of doughnuts or some cheese toasties or a pizza are not difficult to arrange.

  In the session outlines in this material, we have not included hang-out time because the way it works best will be different for each group. The hang-out time does not have to be particularly structured but it does need to happen.

- **Teaching** – in Acts 2 we are told that the believers devoted themselves to the Apostles' teaching (verse 42). The Apostles were commissioned by Jesus to be the authoritative teachers of the early church (John 15:26-27). In the New Testament, the Apostles' teaching is authenticated as God's word through signs and wonders (Acts 2:43).

  Of course, today, we have the amazing privilege of being able to listen to the Apostles' teaching and so listen to God's word whenever the Bible is opened and read and studied. Being devoted to God must, at least, mean listening to his word and trying to put it into practice in our lives. This is why really good Bible teaching needs to be at the centre of our youth group sessions.

  In the session outlines in this material, the 'Bible Time' is one of the key elements to the session. There will usually be a couple of components to the 'Bible Time' – an introductory Bible activity (Focus) followed by a short Bible study.

  For more help on teaching the Bible to young people, please see 'Seven top tips for teaching the Bible to young people' on page 10.

- **Sharing & Testimony** – one of the ways that Christians show that they are devoted to one another is by getting to know one another and by listening and learning from each other. In our youth group sessions it is great to be able to programme in times where people can get to know each other a bit better. That might be by running a simple mixer activity or by interviewing somebody or by asking people to share their experiences or thoughts on a particular topic or issue.

  In the session outlines in this material we have included a 'Talk Time' in each session. Sometimes these 'Talk Times' are specifically linked to the teaching topic for that session and sometimes they just refer to general issues facing Christians.

We have also included an optional 'Getting to Know You' slot in each session. If your group members already know each other really well then you may decide that this activity is unnecessary.

- **Prayer** – One of the most foundational activities that Christians engage in when they meet together is prayer. Prayer reflects our common status as forgiven sinners who are dependent on God. Prayer demonstrates our concern for and commitment to one another. And yet prayer is often one of the first things that gets dropped from a youth group session or from the programme generally - usually because praying together is embarrassing or hard work. If our groups are Christian groups then we need to pray together and for one another. In fact, although it can be hard work getting a group praying, one of the best ways to grow in devotion to one another is by praying together.

  In the session outlines in this material we have included a 'Prayer Time' in each session. Sometimes this prayer time is directed and flows out of the Bible teaching; sometimes the prayer time is more general.

- **Praising God** – right at the heart of what it means to be Christian, both individually and corporately, is praising God. The psalmist overflows with praise to God, so do the early Christians in Acts 2, and so should the young people in our youth groups.

  Whenever young people meet together as Christians, they ought to be reminded of what God has done and encouraged to praise him. This may mean singing together, but for groups that would prefer not to sing, it will mean exploring other ways to express praise to God – perhaps in reading a Psalm together.

In the session outlines in this material we have included a 'Praise Time' in every session, and have made suggestions for both musical and non-musical youth groups.

- **Practical Care** – probably the most striking and challenging aspect of the early believers' life together, as described in Acts 2, is the practical care that they show for one another: 'All the believers were together and had everything in common. Selling their possessions and goods, they gave to anyone as he had need.'

  This practical and material care for each other ought to be reflected in all Christian youth groups, but rarely seems to be (in the western world at least). We need to give serious thought to how we care for one another practically and how that expresses itself in a youth group environment.

  In the session outlines in this material, we have not included suggestions for practical care because the way it works best will be different for each group, but practical care is an important part of what it means to be Christians together and we need to make sure that it is happening in our groups.

Seven Top Tips for Teaching the Bible to Young People

Tip 1 – Pray

It is God's word that we are teaching so we need his help to teach it. Ultimately he is the only one who can open our eyes to understand the Bible and open the eyes of the young people in our youth groups. So we need to pray when we are preparing, and while we are teaching and afterwards, that God would be at work through the Holy Spirit, helping people to listen, understand and put into practice what we are hearing from God's word.

Tip 2 – The Bible must set the agenda

If we are going to teach the Bible properly to young people we need to let the Bible do the teaching. We need to make sure that what we are teaching in a youth group session is what the passage teaches, and not what we, as the leaders, want to teach or what we think the young people need to hear.

Obviously, as we have planned the programme or picked the topics, we will have had some ideas about why we are teaching that particular topic, but when it actually comes down to dealing with the passage, we need to teach what it says and not what we want it to say. And we need to make sure that all of the elements that go to make up a youth group session work together in teaching the passage.

Tip 3 - Be clear without compromising

The key to good communication is clarity – see Nehemiah 8:8. And the key to clarity is knowing what you want to teach and working out how to teach it in a way that is appropriate, understandable and memorable.

Please note: teaching clearly is not the same as being simplistic or dumbing-down; even the most difficult or complicated truths can be taught to young people if they are taught clearly. Inevitably this means that a good amount of work needs to be done in preparation to make sure that you, as the teacher, understand a passage or a topic. After all, if we do not understand a passage or a topic clearly, then what hope do we have of teaching it clearly to others?

Having done the hard work of understanding a passage or topic, we need then to think carefully about how we communicate that to our target audience. It is a useful exercise to ask whether we are teaching in a way that is appropriate, understandable and memorable.

Tip 4 – Good relationships help good teaching

It is generally true to say that good relationships facilitate good communication – see I Thessalonians 2:8. Of course, it is possible to communicate perfectly effectively with a complete stranger, but it is fair to say that, in normal circumstances, communication is easier where there is a good relationship in place. For instance, in trying to work out what level of communication is appropriate (see above) it helps to know the young people with whom we are trying to communicate, particularly in terms of language, illustration and application.

Some things to remember about developing relationships with young people:

- **Make the Effort**

Building relationships with young people takes time and effort, so we need to make sure that there is enough space in our programme for relationships to develop.

- **Make Boundaries**

Relationships flourish where there are clear and consistently enforced boundaries. It is possible to fall into the trap of thinking that being friends with a young person means allowing them to do what they like or never telling them off. Adult friendships do not work like that and neither do relationships between adults and young people. Young people need to know 'where they stand'; they need to feel secure in relationships and sometimes that means being firm in terms of discipline, boundaries, etc.

- **Be Yourself**

Young people want to relate to adults, so be yourself and do not try to be a teenager. Young people have plenty of friends of their own age, but what many are looking for, particularly in the transition between child and adult, is adults who will value and take an interest in them. Many teenagers, particularly if they are going through a period of conflict or non-communication with their parents, will look for supportive relationships with other adults. Interestingly, this relationship is often developed with a grandparent.

This means that youth and children's leaders do not have to pretend to be younger than they are. It also means that when we are putting together teams to work with children and young people, we do not have to limit ourselves to young leaders.

- **Listen**

Genuine relationships are two-way. So, in building relationships with young people, we need to listen and be appropriately honest and open. Paul talks about sharing his life with the Thessalonians (1 Thessalonians 2:8).

- **Do not take yourself too seriously!**

Because relationships are two-way, there is a possibility that we, as leaders, will be let down in a relationship. This is often the case with teenagers, who may not attach the same importance and significance to a relationship, so it is important that adult leaders do not take themselves too seriously.

Tip 5 - Be aware of the culture but not a slave to it

There is a school of thought that says that those who are involved in youth and children's work have to immerse themselves in the culture of young people – live how they live, dress how they dress, do what they do, etc. That is NOT what is being suggested here. Quite apart from anything else, youth culture is extremely difficult to define, partly because it is a mixture of all sorts of cultures and partly because no young person willingly fits into the 'typical' category.

There are, however, clearly differences between the world of young people and the world of adults. But, as we have seen already, young people want to relate to adults, and are therefore expecting that there will be a degree of cultural diversity. In fact, it is often this cultural diversity which adds value to the relationship – the fact that someone from a different world, culturally, is taking an interest in me and my world.

Having said all that, taking an interest in their lives and the world in which they live is an indication that we care for people, so it is worth being aware of the culture of the young people with whom we are working. So we might not like the music that they are into, but we can still ask about it. We may not watch the same programmes that they like, but we can still be aware of them.

In particular, if we are trying to communicate to teenagers, then it is worth learning about communication in the world of young people. Obviously, as we spend time with young people, we will begin to learn how they communicate.

However, there are a couple of ways that you can short-cut the process:

- Talk to school teachers. They are the ones who are specifically trained to communicate to young people. Good school teachers will have a wealth of knowledge and experience in communicating to teenagers.
- Watch television – particularly early in the evening, when programming and advertising is aimed specifically at young people. It is worth watching the advertisements every now and again, because advertisers know how to communicate to teenagers.

Tip 6 - Be varied in communication

One of the lessons from the culture of young people is the need to use variety in our communication. A very quick look at the advertisements or morning television shows us that young people are used to receiving a great deal of information, very quickly. And that information comes in a variety of forms – images, noises, words, instructions, actions, etc. Being varied in communication recognises, as we have seen already, that people learn or take in information differently.

Of course the Bible itself is full of variety in communication. Sometimes the communication is very visual – dreams, visions, parables or exciting narrative. Even as we read the passages, we are encouraged to visualise what is happening. Sometimes the communication is audible – the prophet speaks, the letter is read out, Jesus talks to somebody – and, again, even as we read these passages, it is as though we are listening in to what is being said. Sometimes the communication in the Bible is more physical – animal sacrifice, Jesus touching the leper, Thomas touching Jesus' hands and side, all communicating theological truth physically.

When teaching the Bible to young people it is important that we allow the richness and diversity of the Bible to be reflected in our teaching.

Tip 7 - Preparation is everything

Preparing a youth group session can be harder than preparing a talk or a study for adults. As well as doing all of the same preparation in terms of understanding the passage, you then have to work out how on earth you are going to communicate it to 14, 16, or 18 year olds.

The more time that leaders are able to take in preparing sessions, the better able they will be to teach young people effectively.

SERIES OVERVIEW
SEX AND RELATIONSHIPS

Lesson 1 'Male and female, he created them' .... Genesis 1–3
Looking back at Genesis to see the blueprint for our relationships in God's creation.

Lesson 2 'Exchanging God's truth for lies' .... Romans 1:18-27
Paul's explanation of sin helps us to see that we all worship something and wrong worship leads to a wrong view of sex.

Lesson 3 'Flee from sexual immorality' .... 1 Corinthians 6:12-20
Our identity in Christ gives us a godly perspective on areas from which other people take their identity, including our attitude to sex and relationships..

Lesson 4 'Live as children of light' .... Ephesians 5:1-14
One of the biggest mistakes is to live in imitation of the world when we should be living as children of light.

Lesson 5 'What I hate I do' .... Romans 7:7–8:2
Living up to God's ideals in our relationships is impossible, we fail to stop our sinful nature. But God has the answer.

Lesson 6 'Create in me a pure heart' .... Genesis 39:1-23
A positive case study. Joseph is a good example of 'fleeing the evil desires of youth'.

The world's view of the relationship between men and women is very different from God's original plan for us. Our difficulty is often that we have become so rooted in our culture that we cannot see the problems with it. Sin can also become so rooted in us that we are unable to break free from its grip or even see the state that we are in. What the Bible says about sex and relationships between men and women is, therefore, one of those topics that youth leaders can and should revisit frequently in studies with their groups.

We begin this series of studies on relationships by looking back at God's blueprint in Genesis. We learn about God's good and perfect original plan for relationships. Studies 2-5 are designed to explore four different New Testament passages concerning sexual behaviour. Session 2 looks at what we live for and whether anything has replaced God as the object of our worship. Session 3 asks if our identity is tied to our relationship with God or whether we rely on something else.

Session 4 asks whether we are living all out for God and going in the direction he wants or whether we are trying to get as close to sinning as we can without getting caught. Session 5 starts by recognising that we do sin and we will fail, even the Apostle Paul did, but the session brings us back to a God who shows us infinite grace and willingly forgives. The final session takes a case study from the Bible. Joseph was presented with the temptation to sexual sin when his boss's wife tried to seduce him. His example is a good one to follow.

Guidelines for Leaders

Sex and relationships is a sensitive topic to deal with in youth groups. These sessions have been written in order to guide groups towards some big truths contained in passages crucial for a biblical understanding of the topic. There are many more places in the Bible that we could turn to, but these have been chosen to challenge more than our outward behaviour, to challenge the state of our hearts and our personal relationship with God.

Whilst the aim has been to have a solidly biblical 'off-the-shelf' Bible study on sex and relationships for youth leaders to use, this series should be viewed as a springboard to more study and discussion, rather than a silver bullet to solve the 'sex issue' once and for all.

When preparing for this topic, probably more than any other thematic based study, it is worth considering doing the Bible studies in single sex groups. That does not mean that the whole session needs to be spent this way. However, when the questions get on to more personal issues and challenging application, there may well be more openness and honesty if the groups are not mixed.

LESSON 1

'MALE AND FEMALE, HE CREATED THEM'

BIBLE READING

Genesis 1–3

TEACHING POINT

God created men and women. His original plan for our relationships was perfect.

LEADER'S PREPARATION

This study goes back to the beginning of the Bible, to creation, and looks at the way God created men and women. In particular it looks at the relationship between them. When God looked at all he had made his assessment was that it was 'very good' (Genesis 1:31). That includes relationships between men and women and sex.

However, the Fall is characterised by doubt and disobedience. Doubt that the way God has created us is actually in our best interests and disobedience towards God and his will for us. But we soon see that this leads to a break-down in relationships.

The wonderful 'flesh of my flesh' (Genesis 2:23) relationship is gone and in its place is a competitive and painful relationship that has the potential for destruction. That is lesson one about relationships: God's blueprint was good and perfect, but now it is spoiled.

QUESTIONS

In whose image is humankind created? What is their role?

1:26 God made humans in his own image. It is worth noting that both men and women are mentioned in this context. Not until Chapter 2 do we read that the woman was made out of the man.

The man and the woman have the role of filling the earth and subduing it. They are to rule over creation as God's stewards on earth.

Why do you think that the bit about image is repeated in verse 27? What else is emphasised?

1:27 The fact that we are made in God's image is mentioned three times. Repetition in the Bible is a way of writing in bold and underlined, so this is meant to stand out as important. None of the animals is described in this way.

The word 'created' is also emphasised. Men and women are at the pinnacle of creation, but they are still not equal with the Creator. They are subject to his rule. 'Rule' is the third repeated idea. That is our job and it is repeated to show us that it is important.

Why does God make Eve?

2:18 Eve is going to be a companion and 'suitable helper' for Adam. In other words women are designed especially to pair with men. That is God's blueprint.

How did God create Eve? And how did Adam relate to her?

2:21-23 Eve was created, by God, 'out of man'. She is literally a part of him. Adam clearly thought highly of Eve as he recognises where she has come from and his unique relationship with her as opposed to any other creature.

How are a husband and wife described in verse 24?

2:24 This verse is a very important one for understanding God's original blueprint for our relationships. Jesus himself quotes it (Matthew 19:4-6). It tells us that the right place for sex is in marriage.

Husband and wife are described as 'one flesh'. The closeness of their relationship, the fact that they are 'suitable companions' designed for one another, and the nature of a sexual union between husband and wife is all summed up in that phrase.

The older versions of the Bible, like the King James, translate verse 24 as leaving (father and mother) and cleaving (to his wife). The blueprint for relationships is 'family'. When a man leaves his father and mother he does not go alone, he starts a new family with his wife.

Based on Genesis 1 and 2, what similarities and differences are there between men and women?

Similarities	**Differences**
Both made in God's image (1:26-27)	woman for companionship (2:18)
'flesh of my flesh' (2:23)	woman made out of man (2:21-22)
Instructed to rule creation (1:26,28)	woman is 'suitable helper' (2:18)
Naked and feel no shame (2:25)	

Conclusions

Men and women are created equal and both have the instruction to rule over the earth, that is, to be stewards under God's rule over creation. However, their tasks differ when described in Chapter 2 – woman is created to provide companionship, to be a helper.

Two other important things to remember are that men and women are designed to be together; and that man was created first, his authority further established by the fact that man alone names the animals and he names the woman.

How do the following verses show that the relationship between men and women has changed?

3:6-7,10 These verses tell us that shame and guilt have come into the world. The innocence of Chapter 2 is gone and now there are secrets and lies. Secondly, we see the pro-active role of the woman that reverses the order of creation (headship of the man).

3:16-17 All the established relationships of creation are now spoiled. In particular, verse 16b tells us that the woman now desires to rule over her husband instead of submitting to his rule (the same word 'desire', meaning desiring to rule, is used in Chapter 4:7 about Cain). The man's response is to 'rule over' his wife, implying that he will even throw his weight around.

God's perfect blueprint is lost and in its place is the world as we still know it.

How do we experience the spoiled relationships between men and women today?

Answers could range across a number of very sensitive issues, so be very careful. Things like marital abuse, divorce and even rape might be discussed. The general sense should be that we do not experience either relationships or sex as God first intended.

Do you need to find out more about God's good plan for you and for creation so that you don't doubt it? Think of ways that you could do this.

This is an opportunity to talk about the gospel and to follow it up with those who need to know more.

Are there areas of your life when you are disobedient even though you know that it is wrong to ignore God's rule? What are you going to do about them?

This is again a question to treat sensitively. Bring all the things that are talked about to God in prayer. It is important from the outset to emphasise that, whilst we are all guilty of sinning in the area of sexuality (see Matthew 5:27-30), none of us is ouside God's grace. God will forgive all those who honestly and earnestly repent (1 John 1:9).

PLANNING THE SESSION

Welcome

- Introduce yourselves.
- Start the meeting with prayer.

Getting to Know You

Play a game that involves matching celebrity couples (make sure you check the newspapers to make sure they are still together!). When all the pairs are matched talk about what makes those couples good or bad examples.

Talk Time

What sort of things make up a perfect relationship? You could jot the ideas down on a big bit of paper or post-it notes. You could also interview a married couple from the leadership team.

Focus Time

Either take the perfect relationship ideas from Talk Time and put them each in the centre of a piece of paper. (This is easy if they are on post-it notes. Then draw a spider diagram for each one, writing down ideas of how it might work out in practice.

E.g. buying flowers being romantic giving

devotion — **love** — writing a poem

spending time faithfulness

When you have completed several ideas, look for ways that they overlap.

Or if you have a very dramatic group you could act out a famous scene from a romantic play, e.g. the balcony scene from Romeo and Juliet.

Bible Time

See the worksheet on pages 68-69 for the Bible study questions and running order. Photocopy these pages for each group member for use during the study. You might want to do the comparison question on a flipchart or OHP.

Prayer Time

Divide into small groups and pray through some of the ideas that came up in the last two questions.

Praise Time

Sing some songs that praise God the creator. You might want to choose some songs that have male and female parts to highlight the point of this study about equal status, but different roles (see www.kingswaysongs.com or www.emumusic.com for words and music).

If your group doesn't usually sing then you could read Psalm 8 together, particularly focussing on men and women's place in creation.

Extra Ideas

Invite a Christian couple to be interviewed or answer questions from the group about their own marriage. This couple could be leaders in the group, but they should have been married for a few years and both be Christians. In particular brief them to talk about the good things and the difficult things.

LESSON 2

'EXCHANGING GOD'S TRUTH FOR LIES'

BIBLE READING

Romans 1:18-27

TEACHING POINT

Our sexual behaviour is a big clue about whom we worship, God or ourselves.

LEADER'S PREPARATION

Life is 'worship' and we all worship something. That thing is what we live for, put our energy into, daydream about and get really fanatical about. Romans 1:18-27 gives a graphic description of what life is like when the spotlight of our lives is not on God. It is true to say that when men and women stop worshipping God, they don't worship 'nothing', but anything.

In fact, as we find out in Romans, sex and relationships turn out to be a key way a person expresses false worship. Verse 18 sums it up: 'the wrath of God is being revealed… against all the… wickedness of men'. The sexual impurity we experience all around us, every day, is the result of sin. At its root this sin is idolatry – the desire to worship anything other than God.

The most common thing that gets worshipped in God's place is ourselves. Again, verse 18 summarises: men, who by their unrighteousness suppress the truth. Instead of the truth, we listen to the lie that life is all about ME. That is how we convince ourselves to give in to our desires and to brush impurity under the carpet. Paul does not say that sexual impurity is greater than other sins, but he does give us Lesson 2 very clearly – the way we treat sex is a good hint about whom we are really worshipping.

QUESTIONS

What tense are the verbs in verses 18-19, past, present or future? What is going on right now?

1:18-19 God's wrath *is being revealed* (present tense) against men who *suppress the truth* (present tense), what can be known about God *is plain to them* (present tense) because *God has shown it to them* (past tense).

In other words there is a whole bundle of stuff (sin and God's wrath) going on NOW, despite the fact that God has shown people the truth in the PAST. In fact, the verb meaning 'shown' is not a past tense, it has no tense (if you want to get technical, it is aorist). It points to what God has revealed as a whole. The sense is of the whole package that God has shown. It is all out there, so there are no excuses.

NB Try not to get sidetracked into a debate about whether judgment is happening now or will happen in the future. The danger being that people will want to try to tie specific events together as sin and punishment (e.g. homosexuality and AIDS). This is not helpful. It is true to say that God holds full judgment in reserve for the end of the world. However, we still live with the consequences of our sinful actions, so if you kill someone you will go to jail.

Why have men and women got no excuse for their behaviour?

1:20 Quite simply, God's attributes are on display in creation. There is no excuse for looking out at the world in all its glory and still ignoring the Creator.

What foolish things have men and women done and what wise things have they not done? Can you spot three 'exchanges' they make?

1:21-23 Wise things not done – worshipping God and giving thanks to him, despite knowing him.

Foolish things done – repeated pattern of 'exchange'.

They exchanged the glory of God for images of created things; exchanged the truth of God for a lie; exchanged natural relations for unnatural ones.

Since men and women make those exchanges, God gives them what they ask for. Can you spot three things that God 'gives them over to'?

1:24-27 God gives them over to their desires:

- sexual impurity (the Bible's shorthand for any sex outside of marriage).

- degrading of their bodies (the body becomes cheap not something valuable, created to be good by God).
- shameful lusts (remember Genesis 2:25, shame was unknown in God's perfect creation).
- unnatural relations (natural must mean the way we were created, since this list seems to point us back to the pre-Fall situation for comparison with the current sinful desires. This helps tackle the question that some people raise about their own sexual misbehaviour when they announce that their sin is 'natural for them').
- indecent acts (this seems to refer to homosexuality). 'Receiving the due penalty' is sometimes taken to mean a particular affliction, such as AIDS, prevalent amongst homosexual people. As with question 2 we must be warned against trying to tie together specific sins and punishments as cause and effect. It is better to say, perhaps, that all evil and sickness is evidence of God's wrath over sin, since it is the effect of living in a fallen world. Such things will not exist in heaven (Revelation 21 v. 4).

Is it a shock that God lets men and women get on with these things? In what sense is it a punishment?

You might get a range of answers to this question. Some might be shocked that God allows punishment for sin. They will ask how God can be a God of love? Others will see God's action as just. Some people might equate a punishing God with the God of the Old Testament, imagining the God of the New Testament to be only loving.

To understand why these things are a punishment we need to grasp the overall flow of the passage. The big sin comes in verse 21 – men and women do not glorify God or give thanks to him. The rest of the section stems from this, so the consequence of rejecting God is that we will sin more and more, because we will hate God more and more. Those sins (the 'exchanges' in the passage) will draw us further and further into a lifestyle of sin. This is a punishment in itself, since a sinful lifestyle of any kind will always continue in a downward spiral as the consequences of each sinful step are compounded.

In what way is the sexual impurity described in the passage a lie? (You need to think back to Genesis 1 and 2.)

This is quite a complex question, but it is well worth getting the answer right because it will help us in our understanding of sin. Adam and Eve listened to the snake's lies as he undermined God's own words – 'Did God really say…' and 'You will not surely die'. In doing so Satan caused Adam and Eve to doubt that God's good plan for their relationship was in their best interest. God is billed as the spoilsport.

That lie is very much alive and well in our day and age, too. Sexual activity is attractive to us and rightly so, because it is God's creation. Sex is used everyday for everything from glamorising soap operas to selling cars. But the lie is that we have a right to behave as we please and that God is a spoilsport for wanting to restrict our enjoyment of sex to marriage.

So by listening to the 'If it feels good, do it' lie and not to God's word, we are reliving Adam and Eve's capitulation to the snake's point of view.

Idolatry is putting anything else in God's place and worshipping that instead. Do any of the things you talked about at the beginning take God's place in your life?

These are the subjects that the group talked about in Talk Time. They may well just be hobbies and enthusiasms, in which case you could lead the discussion towards the question of why we are ready to rave about those things but not about Jesus or the gospel. Does this tell us anything about the depth of our faith?

How do you react when you see and hear friends talking freely about sexual impurity, or see something on the television, even as 'innocent' as an unmarried couple living together?

This is another question aimed at getting a personal or thoughtful response from the young people. Most of them (and us) will actually let the comments of our friends and the liberal attitudes purveyed on the television go without comment. You could talk about whether this is because we are not aware of them, because we are happy to tolerate them, or because we do not want to spoil our friendships by being prudish. But when we do this we are 'suppressing the truth', so onto the next question.

What steps can you take to not 'suppress the truth' about God?

For most of us talking about God more is a start. Then we need to get to know God and his ways from the Bible and start applying them to our lives and the other influences on us. God's word should be the measure by which everything else is measured. This might mean beginning to speak up when we used to be quiet. It might mean that we have to be honest with our friends about how their behaviour makes it difficult for us to live an upright

Christian life. If they are good friends they ought to respect that and it may even lead to a good discussion about the gospel.

Are there areas of your behaviour (language, thoughts, actions) that you need to change to avoid idolatry?

This is very liable to be quite a personal question. Do not pry into people's privacy if they do not want to talk, but do try to get the group to be honest with themselves. It might be useful to do an activity that allows honesty and privacy but does not allow for opting out, e.g. the young people could each write themselves a letter and seal it themselves, so that they know no-one else has seen it. The letter could be sent to them later that week or month, or just kept to the end of the series. The letter will act as a reminder for those personal areas of behaviour.

Does your attitude to any areas of sexual impurity need to change? (E.g. coarse talk, acceptance of loose morality, what you watch on television.)

Most of us can think of areas that we need to change. The use of language is a very difficult area, especially for younger teens in the playground at school. They will stand out if they do not swear. Similarly, texting is an interesting area of discussion these days, where initials can be used to imply swear words or unpleasant phrases. A discussion about these things or our television watching habits will help everyone realise that, if they do decide to change, they are not out there alone. The good news is that change is possible because we can do it in God's strength. God's grace will change us, slowly but surely, into the people he wants us to be (Titus 2:11-12). Also God helps us stand up under the weight of temptation (1 Corinthians 10:13). God wants us to succeed, he is not a 'cosmic cop' just waiting for us to sin.

INFORMATION BOX

Homosexuality

Bible studies about sex will bring up all sorts of sensitive issues, not least the issue of homosexuality. This can be a difficult and emotive subject. Like many areas of sexuality (e.g. sex outside of marriage) the subject of homosexuality has the potential to upset people to the point of losing focus on the gospel itself.

However, we do need to hear what the Bible has to say. This information box seeks to highlight some of the biblical principles in play, as well as beginning to answer some of the more common questions.

'What does the Bible say about Homosexuality?'

There are only a handful of places where guidance on homosexuality is clearly given in the Bible, e.g.

Leviticus 18:22; 20:13, Romans 1:27, 1 Corinthians 6:9-10. There are also a number of places where homosexual tendencies are exhibited by characters in a narrative, e.g. Genesis 19 and Judges 19. In both these cases the behaviour is described as vile or wicked.

The attitude towards active homosexuality as a sin does not change between the Old and New Testaments so it cannot be argued that the Leviticus passages are out of date. It is equally condemned in both testaments. Neither can it be said that the New Testament is homophobic, a serious problem Christians need to be sensitive to. By reading each passage in the context it can be seen that homosexuality is mentioned amongst many other sorts of sinful behaviour. It is not singled out.

Some may reject the Bible as being out of date and just plain wrong; others might point the finger back and say that it is just a matter of personal opinion. At this point the debate has really changed tack onto the authority and nature of Scripture. It is probably worth trying to put the issue of homosexuality to one side whilst dealing with this challenge. To try and debate the authority of Scripture within the context of any single issue will make things quite difficult.

In conclusion the Bible is clear that homosexual activity is wrong. However, it is fair to say that homosexuality is treated like other sins: the temptation may be present but we must resist sin itself. The Bible does not condemn homosexual feelings but it does admonish homosexual behaviour. Many people struggle with homosexual desires, just as others do with heterosexual desires. God gives equal grace to believers in both situations to stand up under the burden.

'Jesus didn't condemn homosexuality, did he?'

Whilst Jesus does not mention homosexuality explicitly, we read often of Jesus giving clear, unambiguous teaching about sexual morality (e.g. Matthew 5:27-30 and 15:19-20). In Matthew 19 in Jesus' answer to the Pharisees' question about divorce, he cites Genesis 2:18-25 giving God's designer plan for relationships, concluding that the blueprint is life-long monogamous marriage between a man and a woman.

So just because Jesus was never asked a question about homosexuality does not mean that it is, therefore, exempt from scriptural guidance. After all, there are many other things that Jesus did not mention.

'But isn't it just a part of my nature, like being left-handed?'

In Romans 1:18-32 we read that homosexuality is part of our sinful, fallen nature and the same is true of other sexual sins. When we suppress the truth about God a wrong attitude towards sex will inevitably follow, whether we consider ourselves to be heterosexual or homosexual. God has designed us to enjoy sex in the context of heterosexual, monogamous marriage. That was the way before the Fall. Anything else that 'feels' natural only feels that way because our sinful nature tells us it is.

You might get into a discussion about whether homosexuality comes through nature or nurture. This is quite a big discussion topic and worth putting to one side if you are under time pressure to get the study finished.

'How can it be wrong if it feels good?'

The same could be said for many other sinful activities. Romans 1 teaches that when God gave mankind over to evil ways it really was a punishment. Even a quick look at the medical evidence shows that homosexuality is not a healthy lifestyle, whatever the propaganda says. To follow this up you may want to look for extra help (see page 35).

What's our response to be?

It is inevitable that these studies about sex will lead to the teenager's own lifestyle choices being challenged. Everyone will have to think about their own lives and, whether homosexual or heterosexual, the correct response for all sin is to come to the cross for forgiveness. We must come in repentance and sorrow. The fruit of this repentance must be a changed lifestyle. This is as true for homosexuality as it is for any other sin.

Be ready for this issue to be one that some members of the group need further help with. Do remember to use other resources at your disposal. There are some books and a website mentioned below. You may want to enlist the help of a senior leader or a counsellor within your church.

For the wider group there is also an issue about whom we accept and whom we do not in our church. The church is a group made up entirely of unworthy sinners, all in the process of being made holy by God through his Spirit. So our attitude towards truly repentant homosexual people should be one of acceptance. They are no better or worse than a repentant heterosexual person. This is a big challenge for all of us, especially young people.

Extra help

Pure Sex (by Tony Payne and Phillip Jensen) has a very helpful appendix.
What some of you were (edited by Chris Keane)
What God has made clean… (by John Richardson)

www.truefreedomtrust.co.uk

PLANNING THE SESSION

Welcome

- Introduce yourselves.
- Start the meeting with prayer.

Getting to Know You

Either play two truths and a lie, in which each member of the group makes three statements about themselves and the others have to guess which is the lie. They may ask a limited number of 'yes or no' questions. If the group is large then split into smaller units.

Or you could start this session with a 'share your hobby' time. Ask some, or even all, of the group to bring in some items that display a hobby that they are really keen on. This leads neatly into the Talk Time.

Talk Time

What is the one thing above anything else that you get really passionate about? Football, cricket, computers, ballet…? What is it about those things that interests you? How do you show your devotion to a particular team/hobby/sport, etc?

Focus Time

Why do we get passionate about things and what is the effect? You could do another spider diagram showing the reasons that we get interested in things (e.g. our friends are into it, it fills the time, it sparks our imagination, it gives us an aim in life, etc.). You could then try a different diagrammatic way of showing the effect of the interest or hobby on us, e.g. a pie chart to show how we spend our money or our time, or get everyone to 'draw a daydream' and display the results.

The point is that how we spend our resources (even time given over to daydreams) is an indicator of what we worship. If anything takes over our lives so much that it affects our Christian walk, it has become an idol.

Bible Time

See the worksheet on pages 70-73 for the Bible study questions and running order. Photocopy these pages for each group member for use during the study. You might want to record the answers to questions 4 and 5 on a flipchart or OHP.

Another way of highlighting repeated phrases is to print off the passage (you are allowed to do a limited amount within copyright rules) and to get the young people to spot the repeated patterns for themselves, maybe using a highlighter pen to mark them.

Prayer Time

Divide into small groups and pray through some of the ideas that came up in the last two questions. Be honest about the areas you need to change.

Praise Time

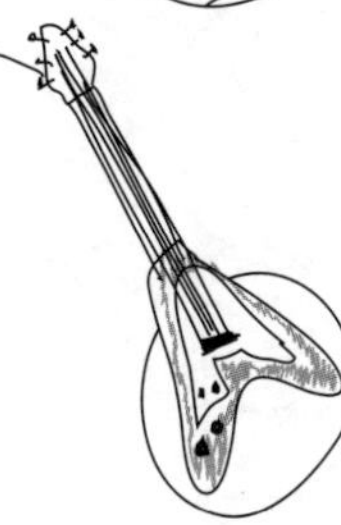

Sing some songs that express sorrow and help the group as they ask for forgiveness for the times that they have exchanged the truth of God for a lie, such as 'God of Grace' and 'Two sins have we committed' (see www.kingswaysongs.com or www.emumusic.com for words and music).

For groups that do not regularly sing, you could read through Psalm 51 together. In this psalm David says sorry to God after the time he committed adultery with Bathsheba.

Extra Ideas

Think about adverts. Legally the advertisers cannot claim things that are not true about their product, but they can mislead us into believing things that are not true. Either show some funny adverts or get the group to act out their own, for fake products.

LESSON 3

'FLEE FROM SEXUAL IMMORALITY'

BIBLE READING

1 Corinthians 6:12-20

TEACHING POINT

Because Christians find their identity in Christ, they will flee from immorality and honour God.

LEADER'S PREPARATION

Our identity, that is, how we would describe who we are, can be bound up with all sorts of things – our wealth and possessions, our achievements, our family and friends or our hobbies.

For the Christian our identity is primarily tied to our relationship with God. We give up our worldly identity for a godly identity. This gives us a godly perspective on all those things that other people take their identity from, including the key areas of sex and relationships.

In particular, our identity as Christians is found in Jesus. We are his servants; nothing else is our master. We look forward to unity with Christ in eternity, so must not unite ourselves with sin now. We are bought by Christ, so our duty and joy is to honour God.

Paul uses unmistakable and firm language: 'unite yourself to the Lord'; 'flee sexual immorality'; 'honour God with your body'. There is no grey area. Sexual immorality is wrong. That means everything that goes against God's original design for men, women and families.

QUESTIONS

'Everything is permissible for me' was a popular slogan for the Corinthians. Christians took this to mean that anything goes. What two considerations does Paul also want them to take?

6:12 Paul wants the Corinthians to realise that not everything is good for you, nor is it advisable to let just anything become your 'master'. Paul does not want the Corinthians to switch off their godly antennae just because they feel free from the burden of sin.

You satisfy your rumbling stomach with food, but why is that different from satisfying your sexual appetite with immorality?

6:13 Put simply, food is meant for the stomach. That is as simple as can be. But the body is not meant for sexual immorality. Those two things do not go together (as the Corinthians were perhaps advocating). The body belongs to the Lord. It is his, so sexual immorality is improper.

Paul points out that God will raise us after death. So who do our bodies belong to now? Why, then, is it important with whom our bodies are united?

(Clue: look back to Genesis 2:24 for God's good and perfect plan for marriage.)

6:14-15 Our bodies belong to God quite literally. He has paid the price to redeem them. That price was Jesus' death. So since our bodies are now God's and are united with Jesus himself, it is important who else gets united with our bodies. Genesis points out that a man will leave his father and mother and be united with his wife. The repeat of the word 'unite' makes it quite clear how important it is for Christians to stick to God's original good plan. This is underlined in verse 16 as Paul reminds the Corinthians that the uniting is how the 'two become one'.

What does Paul mean by 'the body for the Lord' and 'uniting with the Lord'?

6:13,17 To use the comparison of food and sex again, one is not like the other. For simple hunger, food suffices. To fulfil the sexual appetite, casual sex will not do. Our bodies belong to God and are united with Christ, so to act otherwise would be to live a divided life. This sort of life would declare verbally a faith in God, but bear no fruit in a changed lifestyle.

What are Paul's reasons for avoiding sexual immorality?

6:14-17 Your bodies are members of Christ himself, so you are united with the Lord as one in spirit.

6:18 Most sins are outside the body, except sexual sin which is against one's own body.

6:19-20 You were bought at a price, therefore honour God with your body.

What do you think it means to 'honour God with your body'?

To honour God is to glorify him and give him due worth. It is putting God in his proper place. (Remember Romans 1:18 and the consequences of not doing this from last time.)

So, to honour God with our bodies is to put God in his proper place as our Lord and ruler and to let him show us how we should use our bodies. God is quite clear in the Bible about what our behaviour should be like. Honouring God means seeking to please him by being obedient to his instructions in his word. That is very simple to say, but much harder to do.

Paul has used the idea of a temple in verse 19. The temple was symbolic in the Old Testament of God's presence with his people and their worship of him. For Christians this focus shifts away from a stone building in the Middle East and onto ourselves, but the same ideas are there – God's presence with us and our worship of him.

When are you tempted to do things that are not beneficial to growing as a Christian?

6:12 The next two questions are designed to make everybody think hard about their own conduct. Some of the answers may be sensitive or personal, so be careful how you guide the discussion. There may be things that everybody finds similarly challenging. Do not be afraid to go off topic and talk about things unrelated to sex and relationships, but do bring the discussion back round to these things at some point.

What are some of the things that young Christians might end up being mastered by?

6:12 Topics that might come up for discussion are masturbation, pornography, the way we dress, flirting and sexual activity without full sex. Be ready to talk about these openly without being crude. If there is any confusion, remember that the call to be godly is what motivates all Christians, so the answers to some of these questions will not be to draw a line in the sand but to ask how we can honour God in each and every situation. Everybody will have an area of weakness, for many it is in the area of sex and sexuality. Sometimes we need strict discipline to help us obey. Always we need to hear that God's grace is sufficient for us in our weakness (2 Corinthians 12:9).

What makes it difficult to flee? Is there some action you can take?

All sorts of things make it difficult to flee – the company we keep, the way we spend our time, the location of things that are tempting to us (e.g. computers in the bedroom), and so on. We can help by not allowing ourselves to get into situations that present temptation, e.g. not inviting friends of the opposite sex round when Mum and Dad are away. Build in accountability to Christian friends, learning memory verses, finding an older Christian to pray with.

What ways can you honour God with your body?

This question seeks to take one or more of the points of action for the young people and help them to make it a concrete goal for the week. This can be reviewed at the beginning of the next session.

PLANNING THE SESSION

Welcome

- Introduce yourselves.
- Start the meeting with prayer.

Getting to Know You

Write down four words that you think best describe your identity. Answers will range from factual (e.g. British, tall, male, glasses) to esoteric and imaginary. Talk about these with the group.

Talk Time

What are the different places and circumstances where we display our identity? E.g. at school, in a job, with our friends. How do we convey our individuality in those places? E.g. language, clothing, how time is spent, etc. Why do you think our identity and individuality matter to us?

Focus Time

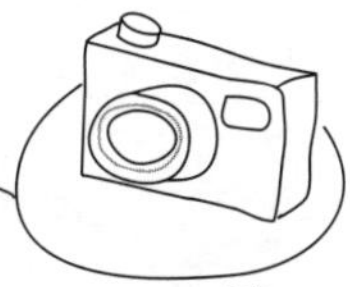

Play a game that involves fleeing, such as tag.

Bible Time

See the worksheet on pages 74-77 for the Bible study questions and running order. Photocopy these pages for each group member for use during the study.

Prayer Time

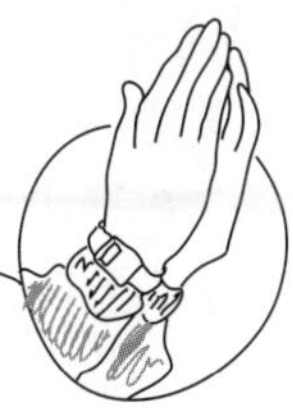

Ask the group to think to themselves about some area of their own 'weakness' and to thank God for his grace towards them.

Divide into small groups and ask for God's help and strength to flee immorality and to honour him.

Praise Time

Sing some songs that Jesus is our Lord and the only right master for us, such as 'My Jesus, my Saviour' and 'Jesus is the name we honour' (see www.kingswaysongs.com or www.emumusic.com for words and music).

If your group does not like to sing, you could read and meditate on Philippians 2:6-11 or Colossians 1:15-20, both of which brilliantly express Jesus' Lordship.

Extra Ideas

Our identity is often tied to the way that we think others see us. Unfortunately, we are most ready to believe the bad things that we think others see. Try this exercise to change things. Pin or tape a piece of paper to everybody's back and give everyone a felt tip pen. Take about five minutes for everybody to write down some positive things anonymously on other people's backs.

Then, perhaps using different colours, have people write some encouraging truths on each other's paper for them to read later. The result is a piece of paper that stops us dwelling on the negative and encourages us to look to God for our true identity.

LESSON 4

'LIVE AS CHILDREN OF LIGHT'

BIBLE READING

Ephesians 5:1-14

TEACHING POINT

Beware of even a hint of impurity; it may be hiding idolatry.

LEADER'S PREPARATION

There is a similarity between the offside line in football and sexual behaviour. Strikers want to get as close to the line as possible without fouling. We often want to get as close to the sexual line as possible without sinning. This is the wrong way of thinking about things. Paul has a clear but firm message for people who hang around near the offside line: forget the idea of trying to get as close to the line as possible, there must not even be a hint of sin.

We probably all struggle with some form of the impurity Paul mentions in this passage, but it's not enough to just say no to the physical things we could do and say that are wrong. They are just outward signs of another problem that starts in our heart – idolatry. The Bible uses this word to describe anything that takes God's place as rightful Lord of our lives.

As you consider today's study do not just think you have to try harder to be good. We will always fail from time to time. Instead try to do some 'heart surgery'. Ask God to change your heart, and the hearts of the young people, so that you have Jesus on the throne. With Jesus in charge you will not want to be anywhere near that offside line.

QUESTIONS

Paul has already explained the gospel to the Ephesians (see 2:1-10). How does he want them to behave because of what God has done for them?

5:1-2 Paul wants the Ephesians to be imitators of God and to live a life of love. Their example for doing this is Jesus himself, who loved us. Jesus showed us what love is by offering himself as a sacrifice to God – that is our 'fragrant offering' too. (See also Romans 12:1-2.)

What instructions does Paul give to those who were 'once in darkness but now are light'?

5:8 Live as children of light (i.e. goodness, righteousness and truth – verse 9).

5:10 Find out what pleases God (in his Word, the Bible).

5:11 Have nothing to do with the fruitless deeds of darkness.

Why cannot light and darkness mix? What does light do to the darkness?

5:13-14 Light and darkness are a good analogy to use, because darkness cannot exist where there is

light. The light chases it away (v.13). Light makes everything visible (v.14), rather than hidden and unseen. So as children of the light we are to live lives that are without hidden bits of darkness/sin, but to let the light of Jesus shine into every corner. That is what the second half of verse 14 means.

Who are God's holy people? (Hint: see Ephesians 1:1.)

5:3-5 We are all God's holy people. The whole of Ephesians so far has been explaining what it means to be a Christian and how that unites Jew and non-Jew together as God's people. Holy means set apart and pure. God's people are set apart from those who are not chosen and are called to be pure.

What must not exist in any measure amongst 'God's holy people'?

5:3 Sexual immorality (anything that is outside God's good plan), impurity and greed must not exist in any measure amongst 'God's holy people'. It should not surprise us that Paul is so strict if you think about the word 'pure'. It is easy to tell when pure water or pure milk has become impure. It will look horrible and taste the same. A Christian is also like that water – any impurity in it is very obvious.

What else should be absent?

5:4 Obscenity, foolish talk and coarse joking should also be absent. Perhaps this list is a surprise because these things can seem so innocent and certainly not as bad as the things on the first list. Using our voices for these things, however, stops us offering thanksgiving to God as we ought.

What does it mean to be an idolater? What is the terrible consequence for an idolater?

5:5 By now we ought to have picked up that being an idolater means having anything other than God in the number one place in our lives. An idol is something that replaces God as the object of our worship. This verse clearly states that letting ourselves get involved in wrong sexual behaviour and language is idolatry. The consequence is terrible – being kept out of God's kingdom.

This question needs to be discussed sensitively. It should have the potential to make us all feel guilty. Some will feel this guilt strongly and be worried that they are not saved and part of God's kingdom. Unless there are obvious signs that they are not, it is worth encouraging the young people that feeling guilty is a sign that God is convicting us of sin. If we were unaware of sin we would not be worried. The important thing is what we do next. To ignore the warning is dangerous. To heed the warning and to ask for forgiveness, trusting in Jesus' sacrifice, is the right response.

Note that verse 6 ties this passage back to both Genesis 3 (Study 1) and Romans 1 (Study 2). The nature of sin and its consequences have not changed, they are just expressed differently here.

Are there occasions when your desire to sin has revealed what is ruling your heart?

We have all had occasions like this. Matthew 5:27-30 reminds us that it is not merely our outward behaviour that has to be pure, but our inner life of thoughts and attitudes. This is impossible for all of us to maintain all of the time, so we must rely on God's grace for help.

What sort of life are we to lead?

5:2 Live a life of love.

What should come out of our lips?

5:4 Thanksgiving.

Whom should we avoid?

5:6 Liars.

What do we try to do in each situation?

5:10 Live to please God.

Christ has offered the sacrifice that covers our sins and atones for (pays the price for) them. So although this passage teaches us some fairly solid truths about how we are to live, we try to do it out of gratitude and obedience to God for what Jesus has already done. We do not do it to try and earn brownie points and achieve our own salvation, that has already been accomplished. This fact ought to motivate us and spur us on to please God and to encourage us when we fail, because God will forgive us. Although we stopped at verse 14 for the purposes of this study, Paul goes on to explain what replaces the old life of debauchery. We are filled with the Spirit (v.18). It is he who works in us to make us more like Christ. That is why we feel guilty when we sin. We will try our hardest to please God and may often fail, but God is at work within us and he never fails.

PLANNING THE SESSION

Welcome

- Introduce yourselves.
- Start the meeting with prayer.

Getting to Know You

Have one person in the group try to explain the offside rule in football to the rest. Give them a time limit, say, thirty seconds. You might want to let them draw on a flipchart, or use figures such as Subbuteo men.

If the offside rule is alien to everybody, choose another game and get someone to explain the rules.

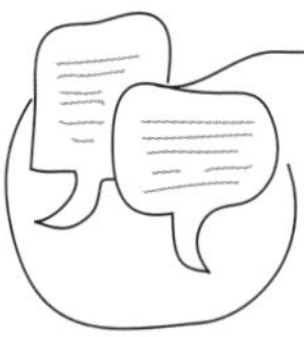

Talk Time

Why do sports and games have rules? What would happen if games did not have rules? Can you think of any rules in a sport or game that do not make sense? Or can you think of instances when it is clear that the players are pushing the rules to the limit, e.g. offside, landing a tennis ball on the edge of the line, etc.

Focus Time

Use light for a game, e.g. play hunt the thimble in the dark if you can black out the room. You could give everyone or only some people a torch.

You could use light to make silhouettes or have a competition to see who can make some animal shapes with their hands.

Bible Time

See the worksheet on pages 78-81 for the Bible study questions and running order. Photocopy these pages for each group member for use during the study.

Prayer Time

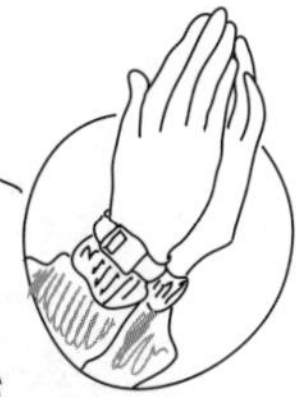

Thank God for the precious gift of his son. Tell God your desire to live with Jesus as Lord. Ask him to help you to find out what pleases him and to do it.

Praise Time

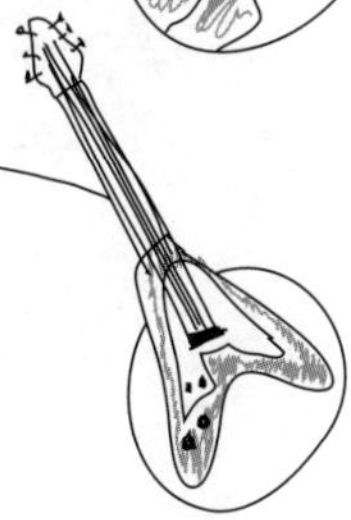

Sing some songs that praise God, such as 'Walking in the light of God' and 'Light of the world' (see www.kingswaysongs.com or www.emumusic.com for words and music).

If your group does not want to sing, read John 1:1-14 together.

Extra Ideas

Using black and white sugar paper, make a light/dark picture. Include a space for a memory verse, e.g. Ephesians 5:8.

LESSON 5

'WHAT I HATE I DO'

BIBLE READING

Romans 7:7–8:2

TEACHING POINT

Our struggle with sin, especially sexual sin, shows us that we need God's grace.

LEADER'S PREPARATION

The game you might have played (see *Getting to Know You*) shows us that we are so conditioned to using 'yes' and 'no' it is hard to stop ourselves saying them. In this passage Paul is making the same point about sin. We are so accustomed to sinning that our attempts to over-ride our sinful nature often end up in failure. This can be especially true for sexual sins.

Our first dip into Romans (Lesson 2) showed us that sin is our desire to worship ourselves rather than God and to suppress his word to us. Paul has made a couple of really big points since then and we catch up with a short look at Chapter 3. All of us have sinned against God, but God's solution is the free gift of justification (being declared right with God) and redemption (having the price of freedom paid for us) see 3:23-24. This solution is available for everyone.

It is a solution freely given because of God's grace. God provided the solution to that war inside us by sending Jesus to take the punishment for our sins. So, although we seem sometimes to be losing the war with sin, the reality is that Jesus has already won and set us free (8:2).

This stops us thinking that we have to be sexually pure before God will accept us. God does accept us and has dealt with our sin, but this does not mean we can go on sinning as much as we like. As we saw last time and will touch on again next time, we are called to live pure lives.

QUESTIONS

How many people are affected by the sin problem?

3:23 Everybody is affected by sin. We read it here in just one verse, but it is the argument that Paul has been building over the last 2½ chapters.

What is the solution to the problem?

3:24 The solution is Jesus. This really is one of those occasions when 'Jesus' is the right answer! Jesus has provided the way for us to be made right with God and freed from sin and its consequences.

Depending on how well you and the group know this passage, you might want to investigate further what 'righteousness', 'justified', 'grace' and 'redemption' mean.

What job does the law do? How does it do this?

7:7 The law teaches us what sin is. It is the marker that shows us how wrong we are.

Paul talks of sin like a person. What does he say this 'person' does?

7:8-9 Sin springs to life because of the law or commandment, says Paul. He means that it was lying dormant prior to knowing the law and he was living his life in blissful ignorance of it. However, as soon as Paul became aware of the law, he became aware of sin and the desire to sin even more was awakened. The sin, at first dormant, sprang to life and started an active role against him.

This matches up to our experience too. Those who are not yet Christian do not realise that they are sinning, although they break God's law every day. As soon as someone comes into contact with God's word, even becoming a Christian, they become aware of the law and therefore of sin.

So, knowing the law makes us aware of sin, but then sin awakes and traps us. What does this lead to?

7:9-11 Simply put, the commandments, which are intended to bring life (e.g. Deuteronomy 5:32-33), actually bring an awareness of sin and even perhaps the desire to sin more. This deception leads to death.

Can you follow the logic of Paul's argument?

7:18-19 These verses summarise Paul's argument but, depending on your group and the time you have, you might want to unpack the entire passage and the flow of logic. Essentially, even when Paul desires to do the right thing, he finds that he is incapable. Instead of the good he desires to do, he ends up doing the evil that he really does not want to do. And remember this is Paul writing, it's not just us that find these things difficult.

What is Paul's relationship with evil? What 'war' is raging inside him? How does this make him feel?

7:22-24 Paul loves God's law and strongly desires to keep it. But there is another 'law' at work in Paul, the unwritten law of sin, fallen human nature. He describes evil as being right beside him all the time. The 'law of sin' wages a war on his mind for control of his body. It quite rightly makes him feel wretched and in need of rescue.

Do you struggle like Paul to do the right thing, but end up doing the wrong thing? Why do you think that this struggle is often worse in the area of sexuality?

It would help for this study to put the answer to this and the following two questions into the context of sexual behaviour and relationships. We must recognise that God's law is good and holy. In other words, what we read in the Bible about God's good plan for sex is the best and only way to behave.

Of course this is difficult and we will struggle – everybody does. However, a Christian will long to keep God's law and to do good. But we are inevitably caught up in the war between God's law and the law of sin at work in each of us. Living like this is part of the tension of being a Christian in the here and now, and not being in heaven yet.

The struggle is arguably more difficult in the area of sexuality, because we are bombarded with images, ideas and stories (in newspapers or on the telly) many times every day. That's not to say that an addiction to, say, gambling, is not as serious for some people. We all have weaknesses and they are all serious. However, sex is out there and around us all the time. Secondly, going back to the previous study in Corinthians, a wrong attitude to sex results in a sin against our own bodies; in other words the consequences are high.

There is good news. It's not just you who gets it wrong and sins again. What or who is the solution?

7:25 - 8:2 Do not miss this final question out. If that happens the group could end up feeling like hopeless failures, but they need not, because there is a solution in the Lord Jesus. This is one of those occasions where the chapter division gets in the way. In 8:1-2 Paul is clearly referring back to the two laws he has been expounding in Chapter 7. Before he launches into the victorious, wonderful news of Chapter 8 he gives us the solution to this war inside ourselves – no condemnation for those who are in Christ. It's not a blank cheque to do as we please. Paul has dealt with that argument in Chapter 6, but it is the encouragement that a Christian, who feels the weight of sin in their life, needs to hear. As we try, and fail, to do the right things, God's grace will continue to cover our sins. It is only when we reject that grace that we need to feel the burden of sin, because then it is ours alone to bear.

PLANNING THE SESSION

Welcome

- Introduce yourselves.
- Start the meeting with prayer.

Getting to Know You

Play the game in which you are not allowed to say 'yes' or 'no' whilst someone tries to make you by asking you questions. See who can go for the longest without saying them.

Talk Time

It is difficult not to say 'yes' or 'no' eventually, because we are conditioned to use those words a lot. What other things are we conditioned to do without thinking? What is the difference between a bad habit and our conditioning?

Focus Time

Play a game that pits one player against another in a knockout tournament. E.g. arm wrestling, thumb wars, or 'paper, stone, scissors'. Find the champion for the group. This illustrates the battle going on inside us that we look at this week.

Bible Time

See the worksheet on pages 82-83 for the Bible study questions and running order. Photocopy these pages for each group member for use during the study.

As with the previous Romans passage (Session 2) it is quite complex, so make sure you have prepared the answers before the session. You might want to use a flip chart or cards to stick to the wall in order to lay out Paul's argument in 7:18-19 visually.

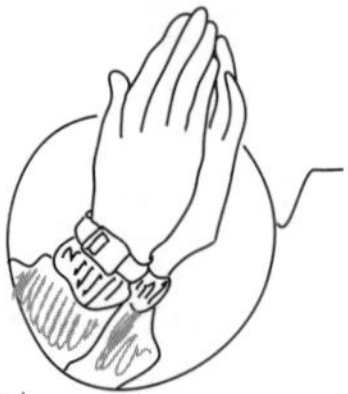

Prayer Time

In your study groups pray for each other as you struggle with sin. Thank God for the grace he shows us in Jesus.

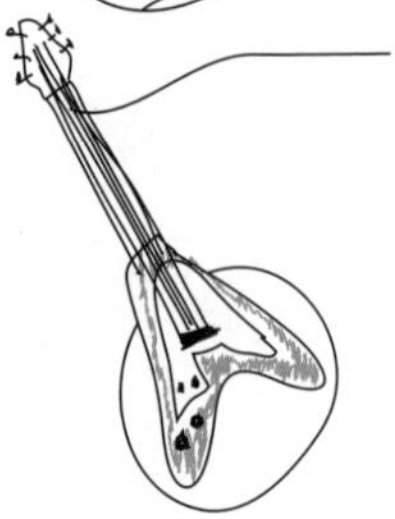

Praise Time

Sing some songs that thank God for the grace he shows us in Jesus, such as 'Wonderful grace' and 'I will offer up my life' (see www.kingswaysongs.com or www.emumusic.com for words and music).

If your group does not want to sing, read Psalm 1 together, focussing on delighting in the law of the Lord (the Bible) as the alternative to walking in the counsel of the wicked.

Extra Ideas

Play any game that involves a battle, e.g. a rolled up newspaper 'snowball' fight.

LESSON 6

'CREATE IN ME A PURE HEART'

BIBLE READING

Genesis 39:1-23

TEACHING POINT

As Christians, we flee from sexual temptation and we pursue righteousness because of a changed heart.

LEADER'S PREPARATION

Sometimes it is tempting to give the young people in our youth groups (or families if we are parents) a list of dangers to avoid in order that they might live to please God. Often, inevitably, we apply Bible passages in this way. There is certainly a pretty long list of things to avoid and it is good to avoid them, but, while strict guidelines can be helpful for wayward sinners, they are not a complete and long-term solution to sin.

Have you thought why we are drawn to temptation and sin at all? The answer lies in our hearts, which is the term the Bible uses for the control-centre of the personality (or of our personhood). It is possible to seek to please God with our behaviour and yet still live to please ourselves in our hearts.

Jeremiah 17:9 says: *The heart is deceitful above all things and beyond cure. Who can understand it?*

Our hearts need reconditioning and training in godliness. This is something that God starts in us the moment that we become Christians and it continues throughout our earthly lives. We can help the process by learning to think and act differently too. One indication of the state of our hearts is our reaction to temptation. Fleeing is a right response to temptation.

In this session we will look at a case study in fleeing sexual temptation. Joseph is a good example of 'fleeing the evil desires of youth', but his reason for fleeing shows us that his heart was right, too, not just his actions. In Psalm 51 David, like Joseph, recognises that sin is above all an offence against God (51:4) and that his heart was the main problem (51:10).

It is very good and absolutely necessary to be ready to flee from evil and say 'no' when faced with sexual temptation. But we can easily fool others and ourselves by merely changing our outward behaviour. God really wants our hearts to be right. In application this will mean drawing the line in a different place entirely.

QUESTIONS

Outline the main events in the story before Joseph is put into jail. How persistant is Potiphar's wife?

The purpose of this question is really to get the facts of the story straight. However, it is worth noting several things. Verse 7 shows us that the bed-hopping antics so prevalent in our TV dramas, Hollywood films and real life are nothing new at all. Verse 10 shows us how very persistent Potiphar's wife was. The thing about temptation is that we have to go on resisting time after time.

It is also worth noticing the big picture. We see that in the fact that the chapter ends in the way it began. Although it is the warden of the prison in which Joseph ends up, rather than Potiphar, who now learns to trust Joseph with everything, God is at work in Joseph's life, whatever his situation.

What do you find out about the way God treats Joseph?

39:2-6 God is with Joseph. This is stated in verse 2 and we read about the results of this in verses 3-6. Joseph's foreign master can see the fact that God is with him. Through Joseph the whole household is blessed. You might want to make the link back to Genesis 12:1-3 in which God promises Abraham that 'all people on earth will be blessed through you.' Whilst this covenant promise ultimately looks forward to Jesus, there are many places in the Old Testament, and this is one, where we see it fulfilled in miniature.

What do you discover about Joseph himself?

39:6 Joseph is obviously trustworthy and, being so, he attracts power and authority in the household. Power alone is attractive to many people, but in Joseph this is combined with physical attractiveness too. It seems that this made him irresistible to Potiphar's wife (v.7) who, presumably, was used to getting her own way.

What reason does Joseph give for refusing Potiphar's wife's request? What is odd about this reason? Who else would Joseph be sinning against?

39:8-9 Joseph makes a little speech about how much his master trusts him and his position of authority in the household. He then declares that he cannot do such a wicked thing against God. This should strike us as odd because, in purely human terms, it is Potiphar's trust that Joseph will be betraying and it is Potiphar's marriage that Joseph will be violating.

Yet for Joseph sin is first and foremost an affront to God. Joseph understands the nature of sin and the orientation of his own heart. He realises that if he gives in to this temptation the sin against Potiphar, which will be great, is just a symptom of the real disease – a heart opposed to worshipping God.

Joseph's older brothers were not brilliant role models. Look at Genesis 35:22 and 38:15-16. Compare their attitudes with Joseph's (39:8-10).

It is easy to wonder why the story of Jacob and his sons is broken up with accounts that do not seem to fit with the flow of the story. In particular, Chapter 38 seems to be quite an odd fit and, needless to say, it is missed out in children's retellings of the Genesis saga.

However, Chapter 38 contains some huge contrasts with Chapter 39, and it may be that the writer wants us to view these chapters next to each other in order to notice this. Going back a bit further, in Genesis 35:22 we see that Jacob's eldest son Reuben has already lowered the moral bar in the household by sleeping with his father's concubine.

In 38:15-16 we see that Judah is not strong when it comes to sexual temptation either. His weakness caused him to seek a prostitute, which is bad enough, although we find out that Tamar was pretending to be a shrine prostitute linked to false religion as well. Judah ends up sleeping with his daughter-in-law, something forbidden in law later on (Leviticus 18:15) and presumably not acceptable at that time.

This is caught up in the bigger story of Judah actually not making sure that the widows of family members were cared for. The culture of the time was for brothers to look after their dead kinsmen's families. In short, it is a complete mess, with poor attitudes and relationships amongst all concerned.

This contrasts vividly with Joseph's own attitude of faithfulness and honesty and his resistance to sexual temptation.

What were the circumstances when Joseph was eventually cornered by Potiphar's wife?

39:11-12 Tellingly, it is when Joseph is alone in the house that he is finally cornered by Potiphar's wife. There are no witnesses and you can only imagine the plotting that Potiphar's wife has been up to in order to engineer such a situation. We know that Joseph behaves in an upright manner, but he has allowed himself to get into a compromising situation, with inevitable consequences when he continues to resist.

It is worth highlighting the importance of our own personal circumstances and how we are often vulnerable to temptation when we are by ourselves. This could mean literally by ourselves, e.g. when parents are out, or figuratively by ourselves if we choose to isolate ourselves from

other Christians, e.g. by not meeting regularly or by having a non-Christian boy/girlfriend.

When you face some of the temptations you should flee from, do you think like Joseph in verse 9? How else are you tempted to think?

We might be tempted to wonder if we can get away with something or not. We forget that sin is primarily an offence against God, who knows everything. Instead, we think that if no-one knows then we are alright. Of course, this also ignores the fact that sin, sexual sin in particular, damages us and our relationships, even if we are the only ones who know about it.

The Bible promises that God will not let us be tempted beyond what we can bear (1 Corinthians 10:13). It is worth learning always to press on a little further with resisting temptation.

How difficult is it to face the same temptations day after day, just as Joseph did (v. 10)? What circumstances are the most dangerous?

It is very difficult to face the same temptations day after day. Our resistance will not last forever without God's help. Sometimes it is crucial to get out of the situation where we face the temptation, in order to avoid the inevitable moment when we will actually give in.

Be prepared to talk about specific circumstances in this question and be ready, perhaps, to need to talk to some individuals later and privately. If you have chosen to do these sessions in single sex groups, that will probably be a huge help when discussing this question.

2 Timothy 2:22
What should we be pursuing as we flee? What sort of people pursue these things?

We should be pursuing righteousness, faith, love and peace. Righteousness means a right standing with God. It is interesting to note that as we flee the 'evil desires of youth' we are not just going anywhere. Actively it takes us to God, who produces in us these godly characteristics when we are dependent on his grace, because we are so aware of our own weakness. It is worth emphasising God's sufficiency alongside our responsibility.

When we pursue these things we are in the company of others who 'call on the Lord out of a pure heart'. The purpose of this study is to highlight the attitude and orientation of our hearts. David's request of God in Psalm 51 should be ours as well: 'Create in me a pure heart and renew a right spirit within me'.

What practical steps can you take to pursue righteousness, faith, love and peace? In what practical ways can you encourage one another to flee the evil desires of youth?

Discussing practical steps will be specific to the situation. As with previous sessions it is worth considering ways of making these practicalities happen and bringing some accountability into the process. Some practical ideas are: writing down a promise, sealing it and putting them in a communal promise box to be opened later; introducing the formation of prayer partners or triplets to pray together and provide accountability; learning memory verses together; or having older Christians in the church give their testimonies.

PLANNING THE SESSION

Welcome

- Introduce yourselves.
- Start the meeting with prayer.

Getting to Know You

Play 'What happened next?' The young people take turns guessing what happened next in a number of situations from films, sports or stories. If you have the skills to do this with video clips, as they do on the quiz programme 'A Question Of Sport', so much the better. However, you could describe scenarios verbally or provide pictures.

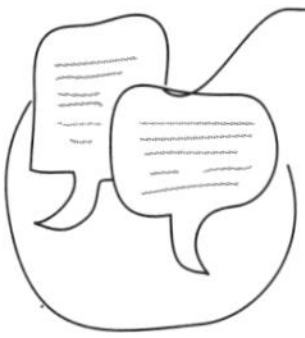

Talk Time

Talk about how our actions are always going to be part of a chain of consequences. Can the young people think of any examples, in real life or fictional, where people do things that lead to inevitable consequences? E.g. Snow White is tempted to eat the apple with the inevitable consequence that she suffers from the witch's poison (although she is alright in the end!).

Focus Time

All our actions have consequences and there are some that we need to get away from at all costs. Read 2 Timothy 2:22. What are the 'evil desires of youth'? Discuss what sort of things we really ought to be fleeing from. You could make a list on a big piece of paper or use post-its. If you put all the things to flee from along one edge of the paper, later in the session you could put the things to pursue along the opposite edge and have a picture of someone running in between.

Bible Time

See the worksheet on pages 84-87 for the Bible study questions and running order. Photocopy these pages for each group member for use during the study.

You might want to draw or write out the 'storyboard' of Joseph's time in Potiphar's household.

Prayer Time

In your study groups pray for each other that God will help you as you struggle with temptation. Thank God that he will always make it possible for us to stand up to temptation. Ask him to change your heart and give you a desire to pursue righteousness, faith, love and peace.

Praise Time

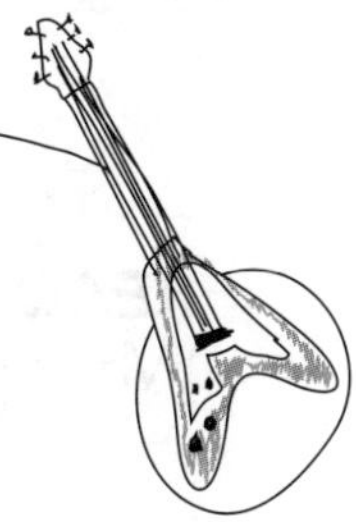

Sing some songs that express gratitude to God for what he has done for us through the cross, such as 'Thank you for the cross' and 'When I was lost' (see www.kingswaysongs.com or www.emumusic.com for words and music).

If your group does not want to sing, read Proverbs 1 v 1-7 together and follow it with one of the passages warning about adultery (e.g. 7:1-12). Use the passages together to meditate about how you can be wise.

Extra Ideas

Life is full of choices. Play the game 'Would you rather…?' which is designed to give everybody an impossible choice between two silly (or sometimes gross!) extremes. No sitting on the fence. E.g. would you rather have three legs or eyes in the back of your head? Would you rather jump into a tub of manure or one of mouldy cheese?

SEX AND RELATIONSHIPS WORKSHEET

READ GENESIS 1:26-28
In whose image is humankind created? What is their role? (v.26)

Why do you think that the bit about image is repeated in verse 27? What else is emphasised?

READ GENESIS 2:18-25
Why does God make Eve? (v.18)

How did God create Eve? And how did Adam relate to her? (v.21-23)

How are a husband and wife described in verse 24?

Based on Genesis 1 & 2, what similarities and differences are there between men and women?

Similarities **Differences**

Read Genesis 3 (if you have time.)
How do the following verses show that the relationship between men and women has changed? (v.6-7,10,16-17)

Personalise it...
How do we experience the spoiled relationships between men and women today?

Do you need to find out more about God's good plan for you and for creation so that you don't doubt it? Think of ways that you could do this.

Are there areas of your life when you are disobedient, even though you know that it is wrong to ignore God's rule? What are you going to do about them?

Read Romans 1:18-27

What tense are the verbs in verses 18-19, past, present or future? What is going on right now?

Why have men and women no excuse for their behaviour? (v.20)

What foolish things have men and women done and what wise things have they not done? Can you spot three 'exchanges' that they make? (v.21-23)

Since men and women make those exchanges, God gives them what they ask for. Can you spot three things that God 'gives them over to'? (v.24-27)

Is it a shock that God lets men and women get on with these things? In what sense is it a punishment?

In what way is the sexual impurity described in the passage a lie? (You need to think back to Genesis 1 & 2.)

Personalise it...

Idolatry is putting anything else in God's place and worshipping that instead. Do any of the things that you talked about at the beginning of the session take God's place in your life?

How do you react when you see and hear friends talking freely about sexual impurity, or see something on the television, even something as 'innocent' as an unmarried couple living together?

What steps can you take to not 'suppress the truth' about God?

Are there areas of your behaviour (language, thoughts, actions) that you need to change to avoid idolatry?

Does your attitude to any areas of sexual impurity need to change? (E.g. coarse talk, acceptance of loose morality, what you watch on television.)

'FLEE FROM SEXUAL IMMORALITY'

SEX AND RELATIONSHIPS WORKSHEET

Read 1 Corinthians 6:12-20

'Everything is permissible for me' was a popular slogan for the Corinthians. Christians took this to mean that anything goes.

What two considerations does Paul also want them to take into account? (v.12)

You satisfy your rumbling stomachs with food, but why is that different to satisfying your sexual appetite with immorality? (v.13)

Paul points out that God will raise us after death, so who do our bodies belong to now? (v.14-15)

Why, then, is it important with whom our bodies are united? (Clue: look back to Genesis 2:24 for God's good and perfect plan for marriage.)

Discuss what you think Paul means by 'the body for the Lord' (v.13) and 'uniting with the Lord' (v.17).

'FLEE FROM SEXUAL IMMORALITY'

SEX AND RELATIONSHIPS WORKSHEET

Fill in the table and complete Paul's reasons for avoiding sexual immorality and the answer he gives for each (v.14-20).

Verses	Reason	Answer
14-17	Your bodies are members of Christ himself, so ...	(v.17)
18	Most sins are outside the body, except ...	(v.18)
19-20	You were bought at a price, therefore ...	(v.20)

What do you think it means to 'honour God with your body'?

Personalise it...

When are you tempted to do things that are not beneficial to growing as a Christian? (v.12)

Talk honestly about some of the things that you might end up being 'mastered' by. (v.12)

What makes it difficult to flee? Is there any action you can take?

What ways can you honour God with your body? What are you going to do about these things this week?

'LIVE AS CHILDREN OF LIGHT'

SEX AND RELATIONSHIPS WORKSHEET

Read Ephesians 5:1-14

Paul has already explained the gospel to the Ephesians (see 2:1-10 if you want to read it).

How does he want them to behave because of what God has done for them? (v.1-2)

Paul says more in verses 8-14. What instructions does he give to those who were 'once in darkness but now are light'?

v.8

v.10

v.11

Why can't light and darkness mix? What does light do to the darkness? (v.13-14)

Read Ephesians 5:3-5 again

Who are God's holy people? (Hint: see Ephesians 1:1.)

Does that include us?

What must not exist in any measure amongst God's holy people? Does it surprise you that God is so strict? (v.3)

What else should be absent? (v.4) What surprises you about this second list?

Verse 5 gives us the crunch. Paul says that immorality, impurity and greed make a man an idolater. What does it mean to be an idolater?

What is the terrible consequence for an idolater?

Personalise it...

Are there occasions when your desire to sin has revealed what is ruling your heart?

If you think that the answer is 'No', check out Matthew 5:27-30 for a reality check.

Hidden in the passage are some great little hints from Paul about positive things we can be doing. Try to dig them out.

v.2 What sort of life are we to lead?

v.4 What should come out of our lips?

v.6 Whom should we avoid?

v.10 What should we try to do in each situation?

It is easy to feel bogged down or trapped by the things we shouldn't do or sins we have committed.

What has Christ done for you? (v.2)

How is this both a motivation to please God and an encouragement when it all goes wrong?

Read Romans 3:22-24

How many people are affected by the sin problem? (v.23)

What is the solution to the problem? (v.24)

Read Romans 7:7-13

What job does the law do? How does it do this? (v.7)

Paul talks of sin like a person. What does he say this 'person' does? (v.8-9)

So, knowing the law makes us aware of sin, but then sin awakes and traps us. What does this lead to? (v.9-11)

Discuss whether you think the law is a good thing or not.

Read Romans 7:14-24
Can you follow the logic of Paul's argument here? Verses 18-19 summarise it well.

Fill in the steps:
Step 1 – Paul desires to...

Step 2 – What is the problem?

Step 3 – Does he do the good he wants to do?

Step 4 – What does he do instead?

In summary, what is Paul's relationship with evil? What 'war' is raging inside him? How does this make him feel? (v.22-24)

Personalise it...
Do you struggle like Paul to do the right thing, but end up doing the wrong thing? Why do you think that this struggle is often worse in the area of sexuality?

There is good news. It's not just you who gets it wrong and sins again. What or who is the solution? (7:25 – 8:2)

Have you stopped trying to do everything by yourself? Who do you rely on for salvation? What can you do to help each other in the battle against sin? Think of some practical things that you can do together.

Read Genesis 39:1-23

Outline the main events in the story before Joseph is put into jail. How persistant is Potiphar's wife?

What do you find out about the way God treats Joseph? (v.2-6)

What do you discover about Joseph himself? (v.6)

What reason does Joseph give for refusing Potiphar's wife's request? What is odd about this reason? Who else would Joseph be sinning against? (v.8-9)

Read Genesis 35:22 and 38:15-16

Joseph's older brothers were not brilliant role models. Compare their attitudes with Joseph's in 39:8-10.

What are the circumstances when Joseph is eventually cornered by Potiphar's wife?

Personalise it...

When you face some of the temptations that you should flee from, do you think like Joseph in verse 9? How else are you tempted to think?

How difficult is it to face the same temptations day after day, just as Joseph did (v.10)? What circumstances are the most dangerous, e.g. Joseph in verse 11?

Read 2 Timothy 2:22

What should we be pursuing as we flee? What sort of people pursue these things?

What practical steps can you take to pursue righteousness, faith, love and peace?

In what practical ways can you encourage one another to flee the evil desires of youth?

CHRISTIAN FOCUS PUBLICATIONS

Christian Focus Christian Heritage CF4K Mentor

Christian Focus Publications publishes books for adults and children under its four main imprints: Christian Focus, Christian Heritage, CF4K and Mentor. Our books reflect that God's word is reliable and Jesus is the way to know him, and live for ever with him.

Our children's publication list includes a Sunday school curriculum that covers pre-school to early teens; puzzle and activity books. We also publish personal and family devotional titles, biographies and inspirational stories that children will love.

If you are looking for quality Bible teaching for children then we have an excellent range of Bible story and age specific theological books.

From pre-school to teenage fiction, we have it covered!

Find us at our web page:
www.christianfocus.com

CF4•K
Because you're never too young to know Jesus